Taurus

20 April – 20 May

amber
BOOKS

ASTROLOGICAL SIGN DATES:
The precise start and end times for each sign vary by a day or two from year to year as the Gregorian calendar shifts relative to the tropical year. The dates provided in this book are correct for the year 2020.

If you are unsure of the Zodiac sign for your specific birth year, visit: www.yourzodiacsign.com.

Taurus

20 April – 20 May

A guide to understanding yourself, your friendships and finding your true love

This edition first published in 2020 by
Amber Books Ltd
United House
North Road
London N7 9DP
United Kingdom
www.amberbooks.co.uk
Instagram: amberbooksltd
Facebook: amberbooks
Twitter: @amberbooks

ISBN: 978-1-83886-024-0

Project Editor: Sarah Uttridge
Design: Zoë Mellors

Picture Credits:
All illustrations by Fabbri Publications except the following:
Shutterstock: 31 (Mount Elbrus), 32 (La Puma), 35 (Slonomysh)

Printed and bound in China

TRADITIONAL CHINESE BOOKBINDING

This book has been produced using traditional Chinese bookbinding techniques, using a method that was developed during the Ming Dynasty (1368–1644) and remained in use until the adoption of Western binding techniques in the early 1900s. In traditional Chinese binding, single sheets of paper are printed on one side only, and each sheet is folded in half, with the printed pages on the outside. The book block is then sandwiched between two boards and sewn together through punched holes close to the cut edges of the folded sheets.

Contents

Introduction

Taurus

20 April–20 May

Sign: The Bull

Ruling Planet: Venus

Gender: Feminine

Element: Earth

Quality: Fixed

Compatibility: Aries, Taurus and Scorpio

Non-compatibility: Aquarius and Sagittarius

Every man, woman and child is born with a distinct and different destiny. There are no exceptions. Everyone has cosmic significance and a part to play in the life of the universe. This is innate and inescapable, and goes beyond the tiny boundaries of nation, creed and colour.

As we live out our lives on planet Earth, we are, however unknowingly, acting in a greater drama and reacting to impulses that come from distant astronomical bodies, stars and planets millions of light years away. Sceptics pour scorn on the idea that far-distant Saturn, for example, can have any effect on our lives, as the ancient art and science of astrology teaches. But the fact is that we are sparks of energy inhabiting bodies made of the same stuff as the stars, responding like tiny radios to the distant messages they send to Earth.

Each infant carries within it a double blueprint for life: its genetic programming and the pattern of character that comes from the astrological 'clock' that was set in motion at the moment of birth. No one knows the full extent of genetic influence, although it seems to be astonishingly far-reaching, but the power of the horoscope has been well known to the wisest men and women for many centuries.

Our Sun signs provide essential inside information about our destinies. They reveal the secrets of who we really are, and why we are here, laying out before us our potential, the sort of joys and achievements our characteristics may bring about, and warn us of problems to be overcome through the triumph of free will.

Read this book with an open mind and discover who you really are.

The Elements

Up to the beginning of the Age of Enlightenment – the modern scientific era – in the 18th century, it was commonly believed that everything, including human beings, was made up of the four elements: Earth, Air, Fire and Water. These were thought of as the building blocks of life, and each astrological sign had a predominance of one or another. Each created its common characteristics, although too much of any of the elements can produce an unbalanced personality.

Earth Signs

Those signs ruled by Earth are Taurus, Virgo and Capricorn. Each manifests the element in different ways. However, in all cases, Earth makes those born under these signs more practical, sensible and stable than most. They are better 'grounded' – or, to put it in another way, they keep their feet on the ground. Whereas others may rush off on madcap schemes or sit around and daydream, those born under Earth signs roll up their sleeves and quietly get on with the job. For example, Arians may be the great explorers and adventurers of the zodiac, but it is Taureans who follow behind, set up camp for them and arrange for provisions to be sent ahead upriver. Taureans are 'the salt of the earth', the plodders who may strike the more dynamic and extrovert signs of the zodiac as being uninspired, but who are invaluable and upright members of society.

Virgoans, always organized, tidy and efficient, are the analysts and notekeepers who keep track of records, accounts and archives so that society knows its history. They are the ones who ensure that the great exploits of the Arian adventurers are known to posterity. Capricornians always have an eye to the future, planning ahead for a rainy day from their lofty mountain peaks, like the Goat that symbolizes their sign. And if they are occasionally dour and pessimistic – thanks to the influence of their ruling planet Saturn, who nevertheless encourages them to be disciplined and careful – then they succeed all the more in keeping the wilder excesses of the Fire and Air signs under control.

Earth Signs

Taurus

Virgo

Capricorn

Colours of the Zodiac

Traditionally, each sign of the zodiac has its own colour, which is believed to be 'lucky' or magically empowered for those born under that particular sign. In general, the colours are associated with the ruling planets and are symbolic of their attributes. Many people find that they feel most comfortable when wearing their sign's colours, and often choose them without knowing their astrological background.

Taurus

Ruling Planet: Venus

Colour: Green – shades of the verdant earth and the spirit of nature. Green is calming and meditative, and can be used to help balance the energies of mind, body and spirit. Too much green, however, can cause lethargy. It was once associated with witchcraft (because it symbolizes the cult of fertility and nature). Consequently, some older people dislike it.

The Angelic Hierarchy

According to ancient tradition, each planet is governed by one of the great archangels, who are also rulers of certain aspects of human life. The box below lists the planet that they rule, the areas over which they have influence and their special day of the week.

Anael

Archangel of Venus.

Governs: Taurus and Libra.

Rules: Matters of the heart, romance, art and music.

Day: Friday

The Genders

Traditionally, the twelve signs of the zodiac are divided into Masculine and Feminine, although of course both men and women are born into each.

The characteristics were assigned to the genders aeons ago, well before modern feminism or political correctness, and may now seem old-fashioned to many. However, the signs do seem to be grouped according to the appropriate gender.

The Feminine Signs

The Feminine signs are Taurus, Cancer, Virgo, Scorpio, Capricorn and Pisces.

Feminine traits tend to be accentuated in the Water signs Cancer and Pisces.

These signs present gentler, more passive qualities. They are the carers and the nurturers, inclined to take a back seat and worry over the well-being of others. They are artistic and in tune with their intuition, and may be psychic. Self-evidently, these are the motherly and sisterly signs, with all the attendant positive and negative characteristics. They tend to be the power behind the throne, rather than movers and shakers, although many are great achievers, especially in the modern, more egalitarian world, where their qualities are encouraged.

Negatively, the Feminine signs can be fussy, possessive, mean-minded, vindictive, cringing, clinging and over-emotional.

Aquarius, the sign of the coming Age, is endowed with both Masculine and Feminine traits, although it is traditionally categorized as Masculine.

The Ruling Planets

Until the 18th century, astrologers knew only the planets of our solar system that could be seen with the naked eye: Mercury, Venus, Mars, Jupiter and Saturn. (For the purposes of astrology, the Sun and the Moon are also counted as planets even though the Sun is a star and the Moon is the satellite of Earth.) Uranus was discovered in 1781, Neptune in 1846 and Pluto was first seen in 1930. Many astrologers believe that the existence of other heavenly bodies – such as the rumoured Vulcan, which hypothetically exists within the orbit of Mercury – is about to be confirmed. Astrologers will then have to agree which signs these 'new' planets will rule, and what human characteristics their discovery will accentuate.

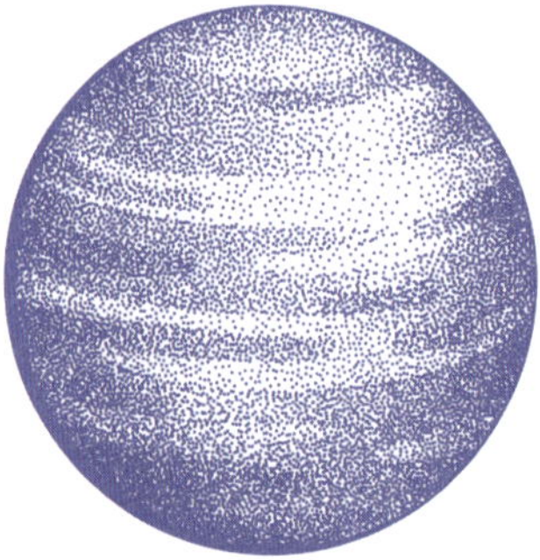

Venus

Venus has always been associated with beauty, harmony and love. The name comes from the Roman goddess of love, who also governed cosmetics, clothes and all finery and luxury. The negative side of Venus is expressed in so-called 'venereal' diseases, which were once thought to be caused by an excess of Venusian influence.

The Greek name for Venus was Aphrodite, while the Egyptians worshipped several goddesses of love and beauty – Isis, Hathor and the cat-headed goddess, Bast. In Christian iconography, the nearest saint to Venus – although of course the Church has never celebrated female sexuality – is Mary Magdalene. In Scandinavia, the goddess of love was Freya, who gave her name to Friday.

About Venus

Our nearest neighbour in the solar system, Venus, is 260 million km (160 million miles) from Earth, and is usually visible at night. It takes 225 days to orbit the Sun.
The sacred day of Venus is Friday.

Venus rules both Taurus and Libra, endowing them both with an appreciation of beautiful things and a lusty love of good sex. Both, in their own way, seek harmony – Taureans, with their need for stability, hate anything that rocks the boat, while Librans' distaste for confrontation underscores all their relationships.

The Qualities

In addition to the influence of gender, the elements and the planets, each sign of the zodiac is affected by having an intrinsic quality – Cardinal, Fixed or Mutable.

Fixed Quality

Individuals born under a Fixed sign have an inherent disposition towards tradition, convention and stability. They hate change and often refuse to adapt to new circumstances. These people are not happy taking the initiative or being in situations that require a quick-fire response. Fixed signs also tend to have conventional, conservative opinions and find it hard to move with the times. However, they do tend to be reliable and down-to-earth.

Taurus

Strong, stubborn and traditional, Taureans are the people who translate the great plans of others into solid, three-dimensional reality. They are at ease with customs that are hallowed by age, and have great respect for old-fashioned values. They are loyal, patriotic and unhappy with any challenge to the status quo.

Signs and Symbols

Most people are familiar with the zodiac 'zoo' – the collection of symbols that represent the twelve signs. These images reflect the characteristics traditionally assigned to each sign and contain a wealth of knowledge about its true nature.

Each sign of the zodiac is represented by a symbol – the twin fish for Pisces, for example. No one is sure exactly when or why the symbols were chosen, although some authorities believe they date from Sumeria or Mesopotamia, 4000 years before Jesus Christ. The priest-astrologers of the ancient world were the first to impose recognizable patterns on the great constellations – Leo the Lion being one example.

Today, seeing such shapes in the stars may seem fanciful, but thousands of years ago imaginations were more poetic, and many myths told of magical animals, such as the dragon, which had strange powers to influence everyday human life.

Although the ancient Egyptians left few astrological records, they were almost unique in antiquity for worshipping archetypal, animal-headed gods. However, these strange hybrid gods – half-human, half-animal – were worshipped as aspects of one God. Contrary to the general belief that the Egyptians were idolaters, their religion was basically monotheistic. Each statue represented an aspect of the one true God.

Since they were established, the signs have remained unchanged, although there was a movement in the Middle Ages to change the sign of Aquarius into the sign of John the Baptist – presumably because of the connection with water.

The twelve signs of the zodiac do seem particularly apt on the whole, and accurately reflect the archetypal character of Sun sign types. The great Swiss psychoanalyst Carl Gustav Jung (1875–1961) believed that, deep in our psyches, humanity shares a collective unconscious – a set of archetypal images, which, at a profound level, we all understand. The signs of the zodiac form part of this pool of images, conveying eternal truths to our unconscious minds.

Signs and Symbols

Aries

Taurus

Gemini

Cancer

Leo

Virgo

Libra

Scorpio

Sagittarius

Capricorn

Aquarius

Pisces

Taurus The Bull

The bull can be wild, raging and dangerous, or content to stand in his field, eating and watching the world go by. Think of the difference between the elegant, doomed bulls of the Spanish bullrings and the domestic British version, lumbering, dull and almost too heavy to move. Although essential to the continuation of his bloodline, the bull does not usually have the sexual voracity of the ram. The quiet, stolid air of many bulls can be misleading. Many picnickers have

discovered to their cost that the overweight beast idly chewing the cud in the corner of the field has a nasty temper and can move like a train when he wants to. Once mobilized, bulls have extraordinary strength and courage. They also have a certain innate dignity.

In the ancient world, the bull was venerated as a symbol of sexual potency and strength, especially in the Minoan civilization of the island of Crete, where bull-leaping was a sacred sport. A sculpture of giant bulls' horns was set up at the boundary of the necropolis of Knossos, where it still stands overlooking the valley.

In Greece, the king of the gods, Zeus, once transformed himself into a bull in order to kidnap and rape Europa.

In Egypt, too, the bull was a sacred animal. In the Middle and New Kingdoms the bull was venerated as the dying-and-rising god Osiris, who was, like Jesus, born on 25 December in humble surroundings. He, too, died on a Friday and rose again three days later. The bull was also seen as the living form of the god Ptah Seker Asari, while during the latter stages of the Greek and Roman occupation of Egypt, the bull represented Serapis, another dying-and-rising god very similar to Jesus.

The Sun in Taurus

Sun sign Taureans are reliable, responsible and affectionate, with strong artistic leanings and a winning way with money. Methodical to a fault, Taureans prefer to stick to well-established plans, rather than change or adapt, and are excellent homemakers and builders of secure families. They are patient, determined and possessed of enormous reserves of strength and common sense. The 'salt of the earth' and strangers to Arian-style tantrums or impulsiveness, they are always there, towers of strength in a crisis. Taureans love routine and rarely question rules, possessing a natural inclination to respect authority and take orders. London, with its love of tradition, pomp and ceremony, is a very Taurean city. Taureans are Establishment figures through and through. Excellent seconds-in-command, they do not often aspire to be the top of their chosen profession, although there are many Taureans who are musical stars, such as Cher, Shirley MacLaine and Barbra Streisand. Natural talent in the performing arts will often take them to the top of the tree, but many Taureans in more conventional lines of work, such as banking or manufacturing, are too afraid of change to pursue the glittering prizes with any real ambition. One of their most typical characteristics is their tendency to plod through life, content with an unremarkable existence as good citizens and the builders of a stable society.

Warm-hearted and loving, Taureans seek above all to create a happy family. Their home is always their castle, however humble it may be. They love to surround themselves with beautiful things, often

Personality Traits of Taureans

Positive:

Reliable
Responsible
Methodical
Affectionate
Artistic
Patient
Determined
Warm-hearted
Love routine

Negative:

Possessive
Jealous
Stubborn
Resistant to change
Indolent
Tendency to plod through life

doing without rather than settling for second-best. Frequently hands-on hobbyists, they are keen on decorating and home improvement, although progress may be slow. One of their most negative traits is indolence, the ability to switch off and do nothing, except perhaps eat, drink and make love.

The sensualists par excellence of the zodiac, Taureans love all forms of self-expression. They turn being pampered into a serious art form. They love being touched or massaged. They are sensual eaters, who pick up food with their hands and greet every dish with an appreciative 'Mmmm'. Gourmands rather than gourmets, Taureans do sometimes become food faddists, seeking out the perfect olive oil or wild mushroom with fanatical single-mindedness. They can also become knowledgeable wine buffs.

Taureans are liable to fierce possessiveness and to making unreasonable accusations, seeing serious liaisons in the most light-hearted and innocent of banter. Jealousy can provoke sudden outbursts of fearful rage, when they charge, like a bull at a gate, in blind fits of fury. Mostly, however, Taurean negativity is expressed in dullness, stubbornness and resistance to change. Taureans can be 'Old Fogeys' at any age.

Appearance

Often short to medium height and stocky, Taureans' delicate hands and feet reveal a strong artistic streak, and although archetypically broad-shouldered, they can have a marked lack of bottom. As the years go by, their lifestyle virtually guarantees increasingly generous padding. Their eyes are bright and soulful, and their voices can be musical and sexy. They move gracefully, surprisingly light on their feet, with the assurance of a dancer. However, they move slowly, in a measured fashion and at a steady pace.

Health

Too much food and wine inevitably takes its toll, and Taureans are often martyrs to obesity and its associated health problems. In some cases, they can find themselves hopelessly addicted to both food and alcohol, although it will

cause them great pain to admit it. Traditionally, Taureans suffer with their throat and necks, which is a grave affliction to the many professional singers in this sign.

They avoid solo sports above all, preferring team games, although many Taureans enjoy golf – that great Establishment pastime. Physically strong, they can suffer greatly from the stress caused by any of the major life changes, such as moving house or the death of a loved one, although they will find it very hard to express their emotions.

Stoical and reserved, Taureans often leave visiting the doctor until they can no longer carry on. Sometimes, this has life-threatening results. Even so, they make good patients, obeying doctor's orders and causing nursing staff no problems. They can be competent, if unimaginative, nurses themselves, and are willing to work long hours at tedious jobs without complaint. Most Taureans are content with conventional medicine, although the more bohemian types will occasionally experiment with complementary therapies such as acupuncture.

Career

Taureans have a wide spread of potential careers, from money matters – accounting, tax collecting and banking – to the arts, building, fashion or gardening. Practical people, Sun sign Taureans are happiest when creating something tangible and lasting, be it a house or a landscaped garden, a painting, sculpture or a piece of haute couture. A fixed Earth sign, they are good at putting down roots and maintaining stability against the ravages of change. If they are trapped in uninspiring office jobs they will transfer their creative cravings to their leisure time, often keeping up several hobbies, from amateur operatics to gardening.

However, Taureans are often content to sit out their entire working lives in dull-as-ditchwater jobs, never really attempting to seek promotion or change to something more demanding. Methodical and thorough, they will duck out of going the extra mile that is so attractive to bosses, and might not show enough of the initiative that marks out someone destined for success. Taureans are the career uniform police officers who rarely rise above the rank of sergeant or the publisher's personal assistant rather than a top-flight editor who snaps up best-selling authors. They are the box office manager rather than the star on stage. Having said that, however, there will be few personal crises and personality clashes in the office. Time-keeping will be flawless and absenteeism will be almost nil. Gritty, dogged and strong, Taureans will rise to tackle any major crisis, from a bomb blast to a flood – their sturdy shoulders ever ready to carry the burdens of others, both literally and figuratively speaking.

The best careers for Taureans

- Project manager
- Banker
- Art director
- Interior designer
- Photographer
- Accountant
- Gardener

Relationships

Taureans like to know where they stand, so they can carve out a distinctive role for themselves that will last, unchanging, throughout the years. In a family situation they like to know where they come in the pecking order, and although they may fume with jealousy over a rival sibling's favoured place in their parents' affections, they will often suffer in silence, keeping their emotional burden to themselves all their lives. Taureans seek harmony and peace above all – 'anything for a quiet life' being one of their favourite sayings – but they can suffer real emotional hardship just to keep the peace. Sometimes, this results in an explosion of rage in inappropriate circumstances, puzzling those who witness it. However, this is the explosion of the long-simmering volcano, rarely having a direct link to the events of the time.

Loyal, devoted Taureans need to make real efforts to keep their relationships fresh. They possess affection, even passion, in vast amounts, but this can easily become bogged down under a welter of complacency. They may forget to speak words of love or keep themselves in attractive shape, or use those little romantic touches that make all the difference. In classic fashion, once married and settled down, Taureans tend to 'let themselves go'. Sometimes, their obsession with their home can make them disinclined to stir out of it, even to take part in family celebrations or holidays, all of which is likely to drive non-Taurean partners mad with boredom. But, on the other hand, Taureans are very generous and hospitable entertainers, so visitors will always be made welcome. Taureans welcome any chance to show off their beautiful home and garden.

Even when ill or out of sorts, Taureans will struggle to do what they consider to be their duty, and this makes them attentive parents – they will always be present at Nativity plays and parents' evenings. They will also keep their children on schedule with homework and studying for exams.

Conscientious and dutiful, Taureans are keen to look after elderly parents and organize the best kind of sheltered accommodation if necessary. They are strong on providing for the future and can be very keen about pension schemes and insurance, and will often be insured up to the hilt for every conceivable eventuality. Though life can be unpredictable, Taureans would rather live without hassle than make a claim.

They will stubbornly cling to a way of doing things that even they admit is long outdated. This can be extremely irritating for loved ones who want to move on to more exciting territory. Taureans are suspicious, even frightened, of spontaneity, and need to be advised well in advance of any plans, even for happy social events. Surprise parties and sudden trips are not for them, and any break in their carefully maintained routine needs to be discussed and thoroughly thrashed out if it is to stand any chance of happening. Generally, however, Taurus is a sign remarkably free of irritating habits.

Taureans make charming company, being careful never to interrupt, make insensitive comments or become aggressive. However, if provoked into an argument about religion or politics, they may stridently defend the belief system with which they grew up, often becoming very heated. They are far happier at conventional social gatherings than anything wild and will react nervously, and with evident disapproval, if good taste is not maintained. On the rare occasions that they do make a social gaffe, they will be overcome with horror and apologize profusely, perhaps not so much because they have hurt someone's feelings but because they have upset the status quo.

Ideal Partner

Typical, stolid Taureans who seek above all to have emotional and material stability could do a lot worse than spend their lives with another Taurean, although sparks will fly should both these obstinate natures clash. They are inclined to be faithful and carry the same values, even the same tastes, throughout life, and so make a perfect match. However, this marriage of similarities may not be the most stimulating, because the challenges they set each other will be strictly limited. With both Earth sign sets of feet firmly on the ground, life will be safe, if a little predictable.

If Taureans want a little magic in their lives, they should go for their opposite zodiacal sign – the intense and magnetic Scorpio, whose smouldering charm often proves fascinating to the sign of the Bull. Profound and often interested in occult mysteries, Scorpians provide the antidote to bovine dullness, but their secretive nature is puzzling to the straightforward and honourable Taurean, and their esoteric interests can upset Taurean conventionality.

Arians, with their fiery energy, can also provide opposite characteristics that create a balance, even though this is often rather tense. In addition, the Ram's tendency to wander, physically and sexually, will not meet with the steady Taurean's approval, although they may secretly admire them for it.

Because of their home-loving and stoical nature, however, Taureans are the best providers of the zodiac and are second only to Cancerians as homemakers. They can, therefore, turn many of the most unpromising relationships with diverse signs of the zodiac into lasting love matches, with few real complaints.

Traditional Taureans can all too easily become worried and upset by those who mock their own values and traditions, so they should be wary of becoming too enamoured of the more rebellious sort of Aquarian – for all their many charms. Nor is the sensible Taurean likely to find much joy with happy-go-lucky Sagittarians, who are never particularly keen to discuss the household accounts or putting something away for a rainy day.

Compatibility in Relationships

Aries

20 March–19 April

Dashing Arians add sparkle to the life of the more prosaic Taurean. They can have long, successful relationships.

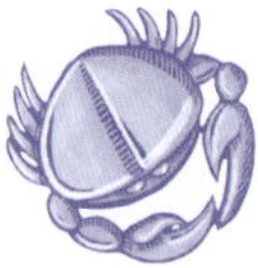

Cancer

21 June–21 July

Well-behaved, stolid, reserved Taureans can find Cancerian scenes just too much to take – but can learn to cope.

Libra

23 September–22 October

Librans, also ruled by Venus, seriously attract Taureans. Librans' outlook is too cool, though.

Capricorn

21 December–20 January

The unadventurous Goat can find happiness with a stolid Bull but sooner or later a red rag will appear.

Taurus

20 April–20 May

Fellow Taureans make for safety, convention and stability. It can work, but it won't be very exciting.

Leo

22 July–22 August

Egocentric Leos often charm Taureans but sooner or later there will be a huge, disastrous – and final – showdown.

Scorpio

23 October–21 November

Opposite sign Scorpians fascinate Taureans but there may be too much murkiness for convention-bound Taureans.

Aquarius

21 January–18 February

To Taureans, unconventional Aquarians can often seem to have come from another planet. No chance!

Gemini

21 May–20 June

Taureans are often attracted to easy-going and sociable Geminians, who can be too daring for this to last.

Virgo

23 August–22 September

Earthy and very organized Virgoans attract Taureans, but this combination can prove too predictable for both.

Sagittarius

22 November–20 December

All that energy and irresponsibility charm but ultimately horrify steady Taureans, who prefer pensions to penury.

Pisces

19 February–19 March

Excessively emotional, clingy Pisceans can be a very definite turn-off for salt-of-the-earth Taureans.

The Taurean Child

Quiet, reserved and often timid, typical Taurean children know how to keep their views and opinions to themselves. This type is rarely naughty and perhaps even something of a 'teacher's pet'. They obey every parental rule, never being too demanding. Yet, they can be stubborn and their respect for authority can evaporate immediately if their most cherished beliefs and habits are threatened. Some Taurean children will even argue with headteachers if they are defending their right to live life at their own pace and in their own way. Sometimes the victims of bullying, they can shock their tormentors by declaring that enough is enough and turning the tables. This is when the quietly grazing bovine turns into the raging bull, and anyone and everyone in the way had better beware! Conversely, another Taurean type can become the bullies themselves, using brute force to intimidate smaller and weaker children, although they are usually too lazy to keep up a lengthy reign of terror.

As siblings, they are often fair-minded and amenable, but their lack of spontaneity and basic acquisitiveness may cause problems in the nursery. Children who are disinclined to be spontaneous and who are inclined to covet others' toys are not the best playmates. They, too, can be ragingly jealous of a new baby brother or sister – being wildly possessive of their mother's attention – although they often react favourably to being given the role of protector to the new addition to the family.

Famous Taureans

Pope John Paul II

Queen Elizabeth II

Charlotte Brontë

Cher

Barbra Streisand

William Shakespeare

Sigmund Freud

Emperor Hirohito

Karl Marx

Robert Oppenheimer

Eva Peron

Sergei Prokofiev

Sugar Ray Robinson

Bertrand Russell

Socrates

Rudolph Valentino

Malcolm X

Bing Crosby

Anthony Trollope

Florence Nightingale

Finding Your Sun Sign (2020 dates)

Aries	20 March–19 April*
Taurus	20 April–20 May
Gemini	21 May–20 June
Cancer	21 June–21 July
Leo	22 July–22 August
Virgo	23 August–22 September
Libra	23 September–22 October
Scorpio	23 October–21 November
Sagittarius	22 November–20 December
Capricorn	21 December–20 January
Aquarius	21 January–18 February
Pisces	19 February–19 March

*The dates provided in this book reflect the year 2020. Dates may vary by a day or two from year to year.